S0-AQC-503

This Book belongs to:
HAWTHORNE ASSEMBLY OF GOD
HAWTHORNE, WISCONSIN

A Parent's Guide To
The Danger Zones
By: Joy Berry + Kathy McBride

DATE	ISSUED TO

A PARENT'S GUIDE TO THE DANGER ZONES

A PARENT'S GUIDE TO THE DANGER ZONES

by Joy Berry and
Kathy McBride

WORD BOOKS

PUBLISHER

WACO, TEXAS

A DIVISION OF
WORD, INCORPORATED

A PARENT'S GUIDE TO THE DANGER ZONES

Library of Congress Cataloging in Publication Data

Berry, Joy.
A parent's guide to the danger zones.

Contents

Publisher's Preface

During the final production of this Danger Zones series, one of our editors related to us something that had just happened in our community, among his own group of friends.

At a neighborhood civic meeting, he had listened to a sobbing mother who was caught in a sudden release of pent-up emotions. She was virtually incoherent. Tears of fear and frustration ran down her face as she tried, with much difficulty, to tell the group what had happened that day.

Two of her children had left home early that morning and did not return at the expected time. Six hours later, after many telephone calls and hours of searching, she still had no idea where they were.

Now, in the grip of her fearful emotions, she couldn't communicate to these people—people who cared—what they needed to know in order to help find her children. Through her tears, she was unable even to describe her children to them.

Finally, a sister of the missing children began to describe her younger brother and sister. She told their ages and hair color, and briefly described the clothing one of the children was wearing.

This family was fortunate. Later in the evening, both

of the children returned, happy and unharmed. They had simply found other interesting kid-things to do on their own after they left home. They didn't realize the potential danger of being on their own, and never thought about the fear and worry their family was going through.

Many of the mother's unspoken thoughts about her missing children were evident. Her fears and concerns were written on her face, especially the biggest one: *What if. . .?* But other questions were there, too, mainly: *What could she have done to prevent this from happening?*

There is so much that we, as concerned parents, should teach our children about safe ways to do things (and some things *not* to do). Unfortunately, we often don't know how to communicate some of the most important, yet delicate issues. It's especially hard to help children recognize potentially dangerous situations and know how to avoid them.

That's why we are publishing this Danger Zones program for kids. It's an effective tool you can use to help your child deal with some important Danger Zones that families face today.

KIDNAPPING

Hundreds of thousands of children are reported missing each year. Over 8,000 of these children are never found. Over 20,000 children are the victims of foul play. Newspapers and television reports constantly remind us that this can (and does!) happen in any size of community in any part of the country.

We CAN alert our children to the dangers of kidnapping without creating inappropriate fear in their lives. *KIDNAPPING* has been developed to help parents teach their children facts and skills that will help them avoid this Danger Zone.

SEXUAL ABUSE

Chances are, you know someone who has been sexually abused. About one out of every four girls and one out of every ten boys will be sexually abused before the age of 18!

The majority of sexual abusers are relatives of their victims. However, there seem to be increasingly frequent instances of sexual abuse committed by non-relatives. It happens in day care centers, schools, camps, and recreation centers. It can even occur in the "safest" homes and involve the most trusted relatives and baby sitters.

SEXUAL ABUSE will help you communicate with your child about this sensitive and important topic. This book is not intended to frighten you or your child, but rather to empower your child to remain safe, happy, and free from this Danger Zone.

ABUSE AND NEGLECT

As parents, we want our children to be safe! We can no longer believe, however, that our kids are safe from this Danger Zone just because neither parent is abusive or neglectful. Many cases of abuse and neglect occur in schools, day care centers, camps, baby sitters' homes, and other "safe" places.

ABUSE AND NEGLECT will help you teach your child the difference between discipline and abuse. An understanding of what constitutes abuse and neglect and an awareness of how he or she is treated can be your child's best protection.

As a publisher, we feel an obligation to deal with the important yet difficult problems kids face today. The problems of sexual abuse, kidnapping, and abuse and neglect of children have existed for a long time. Recent news reports and features simply remind us how widespread these problems are and how they can occur almost anywhere. We believe that children have the right to grow up healthy, happy, and secure. We believe that no child should ever suffer the indignity and the very real threats of physical and emotional harm in these dangerous situations.

This program of books and learning materials can help many children avoid the trauma of these Danger Zones. Perhaps one of these children will be yours.

The Publisher

Introduction

Childhood in our society is seen as a mythical time and place where we are happy, carefree, and secure. If it wasn't quite that way for each of us personally, we believe that it should have been, that it is for children today, and that it can be for our own children. We preserve this myth of childhood by denying the reality of children whose daily experiences are not happy, not carefree, and not secure. To protect ourselves and our children from the discomforting realities of child assault and exploitation, we adults form a conspiracy of silence, ignorance, and denial.

Recently the media have shattered our myths of childhood with news stories of kidnapped and missing children, and those abused by their own family members or caretakers. The threat to all children is real, and aware parents are frightened. We face the difficult process of accepting the painful truth that children are not safe in our society. While social scientists explore the causes and extent of the problem, concerned families are looking for ways to protect their children.

There have been few published resources available to parents willing to educate themselves on the child abuse issue. Parents and caretakers need a concise summary of current information pertaining to their particular concerns, organized in an easy to understand format and language.

A Parent's Guide to the Danger Zones provides parents with the information they need to protect their children. This book is designed to accompany the three books written especially for children on sexual abuse, abuse and neglect, and kidnapping. On its own, it is an informative book for concerned adults.

The child-centered approach of this book requires an understanding of and a commitment to child empowerment. This shared responsibility of the adult and child in the child's protection may require some adjustment in the values system of the adult. The education process, raising the adult's consciousness of the child's perspective, is the principal goal of this series, and of the Parent Guide, in particular. In the back of this book there are multiple copies of each Safety Zones Comprehension Test that may be torn out and given to a child who has read the Danger Zones books to test his/her comprehension. The parent's answer key may be found at the end of each section.

Recognition of victims, causes and effects, intervention, and prevention are discussed. This guide helps parents to protect children by educating them to dangerous persons and situations, and perhaps more importantly, to their rights as human beings. Since only an estimated 3 to 10 percent of perpetrators of sexual offenses against children are total strangers, the delicate issue of children's self-protection in their own environment is another subject of this guide.

Finally, this book will offer parents the necessary tips for the prevention of child abuse and the protection of children. All forms of child abuse constitute a major social problem, the proportions of which defy individual solution. The threat to our children and the future health and stability of our society requires the commitment of all conscientious adults to be aware of the dangers and alert to child protection.

A PARENT'S GUIDE TO THE DANGER ZONES

PART I

Kidnapping

Kidnapping is a fear that every parent knows. The daily news headlines and posters of missing children serve as constant reminders of this threat to children and reinforces our desire to protect them.

The following statistics illustrate the undeniable need for child protection in an unsafe society:

- 500,000 to 2,000,000 children are reported missing in this country each year.
- 20,000 to 50,000 of these children are the victims of foul play.
- 8,000 of these missing children are never found.
- 5,000 children every year are abducted by strangers.

What Is Kidnapping?

The dictionary definition of "kidnap" states:

to seize and detain or carry away by unlawful force or fraud and often with a demand for ransom.

This common definition has certainly fallen behind the meaning implied by current statistics. Few of the estimated 5,000 children abducted by strangers last year were held for ransom. What then are the motivations for this serious crime? And how can we as parents answer our children's fearful question, "Why are children kidnapped?"

Causes of Kidnapping

Child Custody Dispute

Of all children reported missing each year, it is estimated that 150,000 are abducted by noncustodial parents. This illegal seizure of a child by a noncustodial parent, regardless of the assumed loving relationship between them, is a crime of "parental kidnapping." Law enforcement resources can be used by the parent of custody in locating and returning the child. Although the parental kidnap victim is not considered physically threatened, there is considerable danger of emotional trauma to the children caught up in this crime.

Psychological Factors

Kidnapping that is motivated by abnormal behavior is more difficult to understand, and certainly more difficult to explain to our children. Kidnappers are "troubled people" and their possible motivations for the crime are described in terms that a child can understand in the Danger Zones book *Kidnapping,* pages 6–11.

For our own understanding, it may help to be aware that kidnapping is abnormal behavior which might result from any one, or a combination of psychological or social factors, such as:

- psychopathic personality disorder
- childhood abuse and neglect, and/or
- drug and alcohol abuse.

SEEKING SOLUTIONS TO THE PROBLEM OF KIDNAPPING

Supervision

You can protect your child from the danger of kidnapping by providing him with adequate supervision. Choose carefully the adults who will supervise your child (i.e. babysitters, teachers, counselors, etc.).

Choose adults who:

- are in good physical health;
- are in good mental health;
- have been equipped by education, training, and/or experience to work with children;
- are responsible;
- are sensitive, kind, and caring;
- can relate to your children and will have a positive influence on them;
- are people your children can relate to and will respond to, and have a genuine concern for your children's safety and well-being.

Before you get your children involved with an adult, do the following:

Step 1. Interview or observe the adult in action.
Step 2. Talk to people who know the adult.
Step 3. Have your children spend time with the adult.
Step 4. Have your children help you decide whether or not they should get involved with the adult.

No group of children should be left without adult supervision. When your child participates in a supervised group, be sure the ratio of adults to children is adequate for proper supervision. Here are some guidelines for group supervision.
There should be one adult for every:

• 2 infants
• 4 toddlers
• 5 three- to four-year-olds
• 7 four- to six-year-olds
• 10 six- to twelve-year-olds

For proper management, a group should be no larger than:

• 4 infants per group
• 8 toddlers per group
• 15 three- to four-year-olds per group
• 25–30 six- to twelve-year-olds per group

Guidelines for Latchkey Children

More parents than ever are working outside the home. This fact combined with the increase in working single parents has left an estimated 5 to 10 million children, under age 13, without supervised care after school. Children who are responsible for their own after school care have been labeled, "latchkey children." Because they are without adult protection and supervision, latchkey children face a greater risk of being kidnapped.

If you must leave your child at home alone, do everything possible to ensure his or her safety. Here are some guidelines for parents of latchkey children to follow.

- Prepare your child for unsupervised time at home by leaving for brief periods and working up to longer periods of time.
- Decide the rules and go over them carefully with your child.
- Check your home thoroughly for any possible hazards or potentially unsafe features.
- Install security locks, latches, and smoke alarms as needed throughout the house.
- Provide a good flashlight and fire extinguisher and have your child practice using them under your supervision.
- Attach emergency numbers to the telephone or near it and have your child practice using them. Request that a neighbor or nearby friend be your child's reliable contact in case of an emergency.
- Organize parents from your child's school into a "Block Parent" program for added protection on the way home from school.
- Teach your child basic first aid and provide a well-stocked first aid kit within easy reach. Check with your local chapter of the American Red Cross about first aid classes for children.
- Arrange for your child's school to phone you for verification of his or her absence.

- Tape an extra key to the inside of your child's knap-sack or lunch pail.
- Use a sealable plastic bag or zippered pouch to pro-vide an "emergency kit" for the trip to and from school. The kit should include:

  1. an identification card with your child's name, address, home phone number, and parents' work numbers;
  2. coins for emergency phone calls;
  3. the phone number of a friend or relative who could respond to the child's emergency.

- Plan your child's route home from school and make sure it is the same one every day.
- Leave a note of cheer, instructions for after school activities, and reminders, in the same spot each day.
- Do not leave your child home alone for more than three hours a day.

Instruct your children to use the following tips for latchkey children:

- Never accept a ride to or from school unless your parents have arranged it or given their permission.
- Don't go home if you think someone is following you. Get help from the nearest adult.
- Always carry your house key out of sight.
- Check your home from the outside before entering. If a door or window is open or something looks suspi-cious or different to you, don't go inside. Go to the home of a neighbor and call your parents for instruc-tions.
- Have your key ready when you reach your door. Once inside, lock the door behind you, and keep it locked.
- Never open your door to a stranger. Pretend that

your mother or father can't come to the door. If someone insists on being let in, phone your contact neighbor, then your parents.

Check your local chapter of the following organizations for special classes for latchkey children.

- Girl Scouts of America
- Boy Scouts of America
- Camp Fire, Inc. (for both boys and girls)
- Local chapter of the National Committee for the Prevention of Child Abuse

(See resource list beginning on p. 92 for addresses of national headquarters for these organizations.)

Organize

Parents should make their concerns about kidnapping a public issue at all levels of government. Locally, school boards and police services should be consulted about instituting child safety programs in your community. If your school does not have a "Block Parent" program, organize one. Police services may be helpful in promoting such programs, but information and organization can come from parents through school boards.

Block parents are volunteers who offer their home as an emergency refuge to children in trouble on their way home from school. It is not a child care service. Block parents usually live on a well traveled school route, or near the school, and display a sign in the window when they are at home. School cooperation is essential in the program so that children can identify the block parent sign and know they will be offered safety at that home if they need it.

Protect Your Children

Here are some things you can do to protect your children from being kidnapped.

- Avoid putting your children's names on the outside of their clothing or possessions.
- Make a mental note of what your children are wearing when they leave the house.
- Have your children's school call you to verify their absence.
- Direct baby sitters or anyone caring for your child to not allow the child to go with anyone but you.
- Always accompany your child to a public restroom.
- Never leave your child unattended in a parked car.
- Do not allow your child to be out after dark.
- Do not allow your child to play in deserted, dark, isolated, or unsupervised areas.

Here are some things you can do with your children to protect them from being kidnapped.

- Teach your children their full name, address, and telephone number, including their area code, as soon as they are able to memorize this information. Children should also know both parents' full names.
- Have your children use the "whereabouts" forms regularly (p. 113) to report their location to you.
- Make a game out of remembering license plates when traveling with your children. Teach them to

Encourage children to trust their intuition and react assertively when a situation does not feel right to them.

notice the state as well as the number. This will
help your children remember a license plate if they
need to report one.

- Teach your children to yell loudly for help and run
away if they think they are in danger of being kidnapped.

- Encourage your children to trust their intuition and
react assertively when a situation does not feel right
to them. Even if your children overreact, it's better
to be safe than sorry.

- Instruct your children to call you when they reach
their destination. Make sure they have change with
them for using a pay phone.

- Set up a secret code word, known only by you, your
children, and the person who is authorized by you
to transport your children. The code word is your
children's guarantee that the person who approaches
them has been given permission to transport them.

- Have your children practice calling the operator and
police for assistance from a variety of phones, including pay phones.

- Practice observing and describing people with your
children. For younger children, have them use com-
parisons in their descriptions, such as taller than
Daddy or hair lighter than Mommy's.

- Inform your child that adults do not usually ask children for directions, and forbid your child to approach
anyone asking for directions.

- Insist that your child practice the "buddy" system
of traveling in pairs when going anywhere without
adult accompaniment.

- Teach your child about the possible dangers of abduction in public restrooms, including those in movie
theaters. Discourage their use by planning ahead.

Kidnapping lure:

If a restroom visit is necessary, have a friend or trusted adult accompany your child when you are not with him/her.

- Explain to your child that a stranger is someone they don't know. See illustration on p. 29. Then teach them how to avoid strangers. Use the Danger Zones book *Kidnapping,* p. 26.
- Pre-plan a strategy with your child for accidental separation at shopping malls, grocery stores, and public places.
- Role play the lures a potential kidnapper might use with a child. Give your child this opportunity to practice saying, "No," yelling loudly, and showing how fast he or she can run away.

The following lures are among those used by potential kidnappers and child molesters.

- ASSISTANCE. The role of helplessness is often disarming to a child. These requests include: directions to a nearby landmark, restaurant, park, or school; finding a lost puppy; help carrying a heavy load of books or groceries to a car.
- EMERGENCY. This common lure preys on a child's fear about the well-being of loved ones. When a stranger offers your child a ride to the hospital because "Mommy has been hurt," your child can be prepared to ask for the code word, and run away when the stranger can't give it.
- BRIBERY. This is perhaps the best known lure for children. Perpetrators can offer a number of appealing bribes to children which can be refused when the child has been prepared.

Explain to your child that a stranger is someone they don't know.
Then teach them how to avoid strangers.

- AUTHORITY. This is a tricky lure for children because it challenges their respect for authority, and often involves the deception of a uniform. Children should be instructed to have an adult request proper identification from the authority.
- GAMES. This lure is usually transparent unless a costume is employed. Prepare your child to be suspicious of costumed strangers and to act accordingly.
- THREATS. There is little pretense in the use of violent verbal threats, and the child will have no doubt about the danger in this situation. Running away while screaming loudly is the best defense against this lure of intimidation.
- JOBS OR FAME. Older children may be approached with the lure of a job or an opportunity, especially in modeling. Teach your child about such lures and to avoid being photographed without your permission.

To Fight or Not to Fight

A decision all parents must make is whether to teach their children to aggressively defend themselves against attackers. There are two schools of thought on this.

1. By kicking, hitting, and biting, kids can startle their attacker and get away.
2. Such actions only anger the attacker and could cause children to be hurt.

This book does not advocate self-defense for the following reasons.

Pre-plan a strategy with your child for accidental separation at shopping malls, grocery stores, and public places.

- Keeping the assault as nonviolent as possible reduces the chance of the child getting hurt or even killed.
- Since 90 percent of assaults on children are nonviolent, assertive behavior, such as saying no and running away is more appropriate than fighting.
- There is no way of knowing whether or not an attacker has a weapon. Fighting back could cause the attacker to react by using a weapon that is concealed.
- Self-defense training can give children a false sense of security. Instead of being cautious, they might think they can get out of any dangerous situation by fighting.

Runaway Children

Children who run away from home are an easy target of abduction and exploitation. Their reasons for leaving home may vary according to age and home environment. Generally, they are uninformed about the dangers to runaways, and they are seeking an alternative to what they perceive as an unhappy home environment. Running away is often one of the few options a child can exercise over his/her environment—to reject it.

Young children may run away for one or more of the following reasons:

- They need more attention from family members.
- They are angry and feel rejected about a punishment or perceive parents as unfair.
- They are afraid to confront a problem at home or at school.

Young children often leave to punish parents, or at least, to attract their attention. Abused or neglected chil-

Kidnapping lure:

dren are not as likely to run away when they are young, but more likely to leave home in early adolescence.

Adolescent runaways are a highly diverse group. While some teenagers run away to escape an intolerable home life, others run away seeking greater freedom and forbidden thrills. The "acute runaway" leaves home once or twice because of a specific stress. The "chronic runaway" continually seeks to escape the home situation.

One or more of the following signs may indicate a potential adolescent runaway:

- lack of communication with parents
- threats of leaving home
- problems with school, academically or socially
- problems with peers
- mood swings or explosive temper
- emotional withdrawal from family and friends
- rebellious attitude toward authority figures
- collection of personal items, clothing and/or hidden savings.

To prevent children and adolescents from running away:

- Maintain open communication with your child.
- Anticipate problems before they escalate by talking them through.
- Don't ignore your child's threat of running away.
- Educate your child in a matter-of-fact manner about the dangers to runaways.
- Don't threaten to punish your child for running away.
- Monitor your child's behavior and whereabouts during stressful times, especially after conflict or punishment.

Kidnapping lure:

- Allow your adolescent to negotiate areas of disagreement and to exercise agreeable options in his/her home life.
- Seek family counseling to increase communication and resolve chronic family problems.

If your child runs away from home, follow the procedures for missing children on p. 42. Be sure to inform the police that you suspect your child has run away. Most runaways return home within hours or the following day.

If your runaway child phones home:

- Stay calm.
- Ask for his/her location.
- Reassure the child that you want him/her back home.
- Avoid telling your child how worried you are.
- Don't threaten.
- Validate the child's feelings.
- Express your willingness to compromise.
- Request that the child phone you at appointed times if he/she is refusing to return home.
- Express your concern and your need to know if the child is all right.

Patience and calm communication are a parent's best hope of getting a runaway to return home. Most runaways do return on their own.

Fingerprinting

Fingerprinting is an important means of identifying "found" children. There is some controversy about mass fingerprinting and the centralized filing of children's prints. Parents can choose to:

- have their children fingerprinted
- fingerprint their own child
- store the prints at home, or in a safe deposit box
- file their child's fingerprints with a national fingerprint repository

Having Your Child Fingerprinted

A variety of agencies and organizations sponsor fingerprinting programs for children. Your local police department may provide fingerprinting services or recommend another provider of this service.

Before having your child fingerprinted, check the following:

- Where will the fingerprints be filed? Parents should have a copy of the fingerprints or easy access to the files.
- Is your child prepared for the process? Practice fingerprinting young children at home with nontoxic paints or food coloring. Explain the process, what to expect, and the reasons for fingerprinting to older children.
- Is there a charge for the service? Some agencies charge a nominal fee to cover costs of the service. If the cost is too high, consider fingerprinting your child at home.

Fingerprinting Your Child at Home

The fingerprint procedure can be done by parents at home with proper equipment. Fingerprint kits are becoming available from a variety of sources. One organization which provides the proper equipment including permanent ink pad and fingerprint cards at reasonable cost is:

> K-I-D Program
> P.O. Box 6770
> Kansas City, Missouri 64123
> (816) 483–7598

Send $3.25 to the above address for one ink pad and one 8″x8″ fingerprint card. Additional cards are 75 cents per card. To fingerprint your child you will need:

- fingerprint ink pad
- fingerprint card
- washcloth
- non-toxic, extra-strength hand cleaner

Step one: Wash and dry your child's hands thoroughly.

Step two—rolled technique: Roll each finger, beginning with the thumb, from nail edge to nail edge, first on the pad, then on the card in the appropriate box.

Step three—plain impression technique: Press all four fingers onto the pad, then onto the card. Press the thumb by itself. Do not roll the fingers. Repeat the technique for the other hand.

Step four: Clean hands thoroughly with hand cleaner such as that used by mechanics. Be sure it is non-toxic. Soap and water alone will not remove permanent ink.

Tips for quality fingerprinting:

- Be sure the child's hand is relaxed.
- Control the child's fingers in the rolling technique.

- Avoid smudges by not pressing too hard.
- Try to have fun with the process by practicing on plain paper, and letting the child take your fingerprints.

Storing Fingerprints

Store the prints in a safe place with other family records. You need not give a copy to the police or any authorities unless your child is missing.

Filing Fingerprints

You may wish to file your child's fingerprints with a national repository. If so, inquire first about procedures. For more information on filing fingerprints contact:

National Child Identification Center, Inc.
P.O. Box 3068
Albuquerque, New Mexico 87190
(800) 222–4453

Be Prepared

Be prepared for the possible necessity of aiding in a search for your child by compiling an information folder. Make a separate information folder for each of your children. Use a letter-size file folder and label it EMER-GENCY INFORMATION for _____ (child's name).

The file folder contents should include:

- Your child's fingerprints—both hands.
- Your child's palmprints—both hands.
  Call your local police department to find out about
  fingerprinting services. Some schools and community
  organizations offer fingerprinting sessions.
- A current photo of your child (this should be replaced
  every six months to a year). Write this information
  on the back of the photo:

  1. the child's name,
  2. the date the photo was taken, and
  3. the age, height, and weight of your child when the
     photo was taken.

- A lock of your child's hair (this should be placed in
  a plastic bag).

This information should also be placed in your child's
file folder.

Basic Information

- Full name and nickname(s)
- Address
- Telephone number
- Date and place of birth

Physical Information

- Sex
- Nationality/Race
- Height and weight

- Hair color
- Color of eyes
- Complexion color
- Identification marks (scars, birthmarks, tatoos, pierced ears, etc.)
- Physical handicaps
- Past injuries (broken bones, amputations, operations, etc.)
- Allergies
- Is your child right- or left-handed?
- Does your child wear glasses or contact lenses?
- Are any of your child's teeth false or missing?
- Does your child wear braces?

Other Information

- Habits
- Daily activities
- Likes
- Dislikes

General Social Information

Include the names, addresses, and telephone numbers of the following:

- Parents
- Relatives
- Close friends
- Neighbors
- Doctor (to be contacted for medical records)
- Dentist (to be contacted for dental records)

Include the name, addresses, and dates of attendance of the following:

* Schools attended
* Churches attended

What to Do if Your Child Is Missing

Situations will vary depending on the age of the child and other factors, but in general try to remain calm and do the following:

* Look inside your house (check all closets, enclosed spaces, etc.).
* Look around the area immediately surrounding your house.
* Contact the police or sheriff.
* Enlist neighbors to check the neighborhood surrounding your house. Searchers should repeatedly call out the child's name as they look around. Check the child's room for any clues to indicate where the child might be.
* Have someone call your child's friends and ask when they last saw the missing child.
* When the police arrive, give them the emergency information folder and answer all of their questions completely. Alert them to any problems that might have caused your child to run away.
* Have someone stay by your phone during the time your child is missing.
* Call the National Center for Missing Children to report a missing child, or the sighting of a missing child: (800) 843–5678.

Keeping Your Child Safe

Promote an attitude of empowerment in your children by allowing them to be responsible for their own safety. Assuming this responsibility requires the kind of information and skills contained in the Danger Zones book *Kidnapping*. To maximize the book's benefits for your child, do the following:

- Read the book with your child.
- Listen for questions, concerns, and responses to the material.
- Answer your child's questions with a confident, matter-of-fact attitude.

Whereabouts Form

WHERE ARE YOU, _____ ?
(child's name)

Today is: Mon. Tues. Wed. Thurs. Fri. Sat. Sun.
the _____ day of _____ , 19 _____ .

When did you leave (time)? _____

Where will you be? _____

Phone _____

How will you get there?
Walk _____ Ride your bike _____ Car _____ Bus _____

Who will take you? _____

Who will pick you up? _____

Who is with you? _____

How are you returning? _____

When will you be home? _____

Safety Zones Comprehension Test
(Parent's Answer Key)

Part I—Kidnapping

1. Name three of the ways kidnappers might try to trick children into going with them.
   1. Bribes: offering candy, money or surprises, gifts, trips to special places.
   2. Tricks: "I'm lost." "Your parents sent me." "Your parents are hurt."
   3. Intimidation: threatening them.
   4. Force: overpowering them.
2. If you are lost or separated from your parents, what should you do? Find a trustworthy adult and ask for help.
3. If you are separated from your parents and someone is helping you, what information should you give them? Your full name, your address, your telephone number (including area code), your parents' or guardians' full names, the names and addresses of their places of work, and their telephone numbers.
4. What should you do before you leave home? Tell your parents where you will be, what you will be doing, how you will get there, and when you will return.
5. If you decide to go somewhere else on the way to where your parents think you are going, what should you do? Call your parents and tell them where you are.
6. If you think you will return home later than your parents are expecting you, what should you do? Call your parents and tell them you will be late and what time they can expect you to arrive home.
7. What is a stranger? A person you do not know.
8. If a telephone caller wants to speak to your mom or dad and you are home alone, what should you say? "My mother (father) can not come to the phone right now. Can I take a message?"

PART II

Sexual Abuse

The sexual abuse of children is receiving widespread publicity. The recent explosion of information reveals one of our society's best-kept secrets. As the extent of sexual abuse becomes known and the public awareness increases, parents are faced with a threatening reality. How can we keep our children safe from sexual abuse? We need information and a plan of action aimed at prevention.

What Is Sexual Abuse?

Sexual abuse has a very broad definition, the legal terms of which can vary considerably from state to state. The National Center on Child Abuse and Neglect has adopted the following definition in 1981 to include all forms of sexual abuse:

> Contacts or interactions between a child and an adult when the child is being used for the sexual stimulation of that adult or another person. Sexual abuse may also be committed by a person under the age of 18 when that person is either significantly older than the victim or when the abuser is in a position of power or control over another child.

The significance of this definition is its focus on the intention of the abuser rather than on the behavior that was exhibited or its effect on the victim.

Sexual abuse may include (but is not limited to) the following behaviors:

- sexual molestation—sexual contact, such as fondling and exposure
- rape—forced vaginal or anal intercourse
- incest—sexual intercourse between a child and a related adult, usually a parent
- sexual victimization—sexual activity between a child under 12 and a partner at least five years older, or between a child 13 to 16 with a partner at least 10 years older
- sexual exploitation—photographing, video taping, filming, or depicting a child or children in sexually explicit postures for the purpose of the sexual stimulation of adults. This includes child prostitution and child pornography

Extent of the Problem

Victims of sexual abuse represent every race and economic status. Accurate numbers of victims are impossible to determine on a national scale due to:

One out of every five victims of sexual abuse is a child under the age of seven.

1. a lack of reporting
2. failure to compile national statistics from local sources.

The FBI estimates that only one crime of sexual abuse is reported for every five committed. Sexual abuse has been called the most underreported serious crime in the country.

Research conducted by various social scientists have provided the following *estimates* regarding the scope of the problem:

- Of all crimes against children, 75 percent are sexual in nature. Between 100,000 and 500,000 American children will be molested this year.
- National estimates predict a child is being sexually abused somewhere in the U.S. every two minutes.
- One in every five victims of sexual abuse is a child under the age of seven.
- Studies based on the recollections of adults estimate that 52 percent of the women and 9 percent of the men were sexually abused as children.
- One out of every four girls and one out of every ten boys will be sexually abused before they reach the age of eighteen

Who Are the Victims?

All children are potential victims of sexual abuse. Girls are two to ten times more often the target than boys. Children who are abused or neglected at home are more vulnerable to child molesters because they are physically and emotionally needy. Runaway children are a target population for sexual exploitation including the multimillion dollar businesses of child pornography and child prostitution. These forms of abuse have only recently come under investigation by authorities. Juvenile delinquency experts estimate the number of male and female prostitutes under the age of sixteen exceeds 600,000. Justice Department statistics estimate that 85 percent of all children being exploited were missing at the time of exploitation. The growth of child pornography and child prostitution poses a continuing threat of sexual exploitation to children.

Effects of Sexual Abuse on the Victim

The effects of sexual abuse are as difficult to measure as the incidence of the crime. The severity of the effects is relative to the degree of trauma associated with the crime. Death is the most serious effect of sexual abuse, but is rarely the result of sexual assault itself. Often, the effects of sexual abuse are demonstrations of the victim's coping mechanism. Severe effects include those common to the post-traumatic stress disorder of combat veterans. Research indicates that severe trauma of sexual abuse can result in the development of multiple personalities. Physical damage is more visible, easier to treat and quicker to heal than the psychological damage which can result from sexual abuse. The following factors will help to determine the way a child reacts to and assimilates the abuse experience:

- the child's age and developmental stage
- the child's relationship to the abuser
- the amount of force or violence used
- the degree of shame or guilt felt by the child for participation
- the reactions of parents and professionals

Other factors being equal, the degree of trauma is greater when the perpetrator is close to the child than when he is a stranger.

In the absence of force or violence, with other factors being equal, the degree of trauma is greater when the perpetrator is close to the child than when he is a stranger.

CAUSES OF SEXUAL ABUSE

Who Are the Perpetrators?

There is no way to accurately describe the "average" child molester. Contrary to the popular image of the derelict in a raincoat, sex offenders are representative of every social class, race, and religion. The following statistical summaries provide a very general profile of the sexual abuser:

- the overwhelming majority are men;
- 92% are heterosexual;
- 3% to 10% are total strangers to their victim;
- 80% of victims are assaulted by someone they know and trust;
- 80% were sexually abused themselves as children.

Sexual molesters of children are generally classified into two categories:

1. pedophiles
2. regressed offenders

Pedophilia

Pedophilia is an addictive phenomenon in which children are the preferred sexual object. Behavior associated

Eighty percent of victims of sexual abuse are assaulted by someone they know and trust.

with pedophilia can range from photo collecting fantasy to child molesting. Whether or not a child molester identifies with or denies the label of pedophile, this phenomenon poses a threat to children for the following reasons:

- The addictive nature of pedophilia makes the pedophile a predator on children.
- In one study, child molesters were responsible for an average of sixty-eight child molestations each. Recorded tallies for individual offenders are much higher.
- Pedophiles constitute a deviant subculture that spends an estimated 500 million dollars annually on child pornography, a byproduct of child molestation.
- Fewer than 1 percent of child molesters are sent to jail.

Regressed Offenders

The regressed child molester is typically a male under stress who seeks sexual involvement with a non-threatening partner, usually of the opposite sex and past puberty. Alcohol and drug abuse appear to have some impact on this regressive tendency.

Treatment involving behavior control appears to have more positive results with the regressed offender than with the admitted pedophile. Pedophiles themselves claim there is no cure for their addiction. Some pedophiles have formed organizations which attempt to legitimize their sexual behavior by claiming pedophilia as a lifestyle choice.

Pedophiles spend an estimated 500 million dollars annually on child pornography.

Potential Victims

Lack of Supervision

Child protection in this society has diminished with the disappearance of the extended family and the increased pressures on the nuclear family. More parents than ever are working outside the home. Full-time child care and decreased adult supervision are facts of life for many families. For other troubled or disrupted families, children may be needy and unsupervised, presenting a particularly vulnerable target population for child molesters.

Child's Self-Image

The child's internalized attitude about him/herself can also be a pre-disposition to sexual abuse. Children whose behavior indicates high self-esteem and strong self-confidence are generally less vulnerable to sexual abuse.

SEEKING SOLUTIONS TO THE PROBLEMS OF SEXUAL ABUSE

In order to approach the crime of sexual abuse as a social problem, it must be introduced into public awareness. The media are helping to expose the scope of the problem of sexual abuse. This awareness carries with it a social responsibility to protect any child being sexually abused. This protection is best achieved by initiating the legal process which includes the following steps:

1. reporting the crime
2. investigation of the crime

3. intervention for the victim
4. treatment and/or prosecution for the perpetrator

Reporting the Crime

Although procedures vary from state to state, protection of the victim is the goal of law enforcement and child protective services nationwide. Anyone wishing to report a suspected case of sexual abuse should contact one of the following agencies:

1. local police or county sheriff's department
2. the local county welfare department or child protective service which may also be called:

   • Human Resources Agency
   • Department of Public Social Services
   • Department of Health and Human Services
   • Department of Public Assistance

3. the local county juvenile probation department
4. the local child abuse and neglect hot line (if one is established) council or center
5. the local rape crisis center

Reports can be made anonymously, however, investigation is aided when the reporter is identified. In most states, all names are confidential and can be released only by court order.

Investigation and Intervention

The processes of investigation and intervention, where necessary, begin after a case of child sexual abuse is reported. Qualified and experienced child protective authorities can then move to determine the nature of the problem, and intervene for the victim's safety, if necessary.

Treatment and Prosecution

In many cases of sexual abuse, a threat of prosecution is the only incentive for the accused offender to seek treatment. In incest cases, family treatment programs have proven to be an effective alternative to prosecution. Because sexual abuse is an escalating syndrome (incidences tend to increase in frequency and degree), treatment or prosecution is essential for the protection of future victims.

What to Do When Children Are Sexually Abused

If you suspect that your child has been sexually abused, be aware of how your feelings can affect your child by either contributing to the trauma or beginning the healing process. Do the following:

- Request information by asking open-ended questions, or using statements such as, "Describe what happened" rather than leading questions requiring a yes or no answer such as, "Did he hurt you?"
- Make mental or written notes as you gather information on the incident.
- Listen to your child's report in a calm manner. Try not to communicate your own feelings of horror, fear, or anger, which might be misinterpreted as being directed at the victim, rather than the abuser.

Believe your child. Children do not lie about sexual abuse.

- Believe your child. Children do not lie about sexual abuse.
- Beware of placing blame directly or indirectly on the victim, e.g., "If only you had come straight home."
- Communicate total support, comfort, and reassurance that the child has done nothing wrong; that telling was the right thing to do; and that no harm will come from the abuser or anyone else because of telling.
- Oppose the abuser. Let the child know that the abuser was wrong, and that you intend to take appropriate action.
- Follow through by reporting the abuse to the proper authorities. If the abuser is a member of the family, take action by contacting one of the social service agencies listed on pp. 92–112.
- Get medical help. Even when the effects of the abuse do not appear serious, medical examination and documentation as soon as possible after the incident can be vital to a successful prosecution. If possible, choose a physician or medical practitioner who is familiar to the child. Prepare the medical personnel for a sexual abuse case with an advance phone call.
- Seek legal aid for the victim's protection in the event of prosecution.
- Arrange for counseling for both parents and child.

Prevention of Sexual Abuse

Adequate Supervision

Screen all persons who spend time with your child. When you leave your child in the care of another person, their selection requires extreme caution. Follow the guidelines for selecting adult supervision for your child in Part I, page 19. To evaluate a child care facility for your child, use the following suggestions offered by child care agencies:

- Ask to see the day care center's license. Accept no excuses, such as, "It's being mailed to us."
- Obtain a list of other parents whose children stay at the center, and call them for their evaluation. Keep in touch with other parents for continued evaluation.
- Arrange to meet all employees, and ask about volunteers or part-time employees whom you may not have met.
- Check on the following:

  1. Are you comfortable with the kind and degree of affection exchanged between children and caretakers?
  2. How are children put down for their naps?
  3. Are all areas on the premises open to your inspection?

- Observe playtime activities. Watch for acting out behavior of a sexual nature.
- Ask about the center's policies on children's nudity. Then decide if it is acceptable to you.
- Pay a surprise visit to the center and observe the adult/child interaction, and more importantly, the adult response to your presence.
- Question your child regularly about his/her child care center experience.

Parental Awareness

Recognition that the possibility of sexual abuse exists is the first step toward preventing it. Open communica-

Children need a basic understanding of male and female anatomy, and the vocabulary to ask questions about and discuss their own bodies.

tion with your child is one of the most important preventive measures against sexual abuse. Be aware of any changes in your child's behavior. Watch for signs that may indicate sexual abuse. These include:

- regressive behavior, such as thumbsucking or bedwetting
- nightmares or sleep disturbances
- loss of appetite
- extreme anxiety symptoms
- expressed fear of going to child care or associating with a particular person
- change in attitude or performance in school
- physical signs, such as: redness around the genital area, genital irritation, underpants worn inside out, genital or rectal bleeding, or unexplained bruises

Child Protection

Education is your child's best defense against sexual abuse. Teach your child the following:

- Physical autonomy. Our bodies are private, and no one has a right to invade that private zone.
- Appropriate touches. There are good, appropriate touches, and inappropriate touches that feel different.
- To trust his or her instincts about a person or situation, and to act on those instincts.
- Assertive behavior. Every child has a right to say no. There are many ways to say no, so have your

Teach your child to trust his or her instincts about a person or situation, and to act on those instincts.

child practice saying it in different ways. Examples are:

"Don't do that!"
"I don't want to."
"I'm not supposed to do this."
"I'm going to tell on you if you don't stop."

In many cases, the child's firm refusal to participate is a strong enough deterrent to stop the abuse attempt.

- To tell you about any questionable activity with another person. Make yourself accessible for disclosure, and encourage your child not to keep secrets from you.
- Human anatomy and sexuality appropriate to the child's development. Children need a basic understanding of male and female anatomy, and the appropriate vocabulary to ask questions about and discuss their own bodies.

Since abduction is sometimes used by child molesters, follow the guidelines presented in Part I to protect your child from abduction, p. 24.

Children's self protection against sexual abuse is presented in *Danger Zones: Alerting Your Child to the Dangers of Sexual Abuse*. To maximize the book's benefits for your child, do the following:

- Read the book with your child.
- Listen for questions, concerns, and responses to the material.
- Answer your child's questions with a confident, matter-of-fact attitude.

In many cases, the child's firm refusal to participate is a strong enough deterrent to stop the abuse attempt.

Safety Zones Comprehension Test
(Parent's Answer Key)

Part II—Sexual Abuse

1. Describe three of the ways a sexual abuser might get a victim to cooperate.

1 Friendship	5 Tricks
2 Withholding	6 Intimidation
3 Bribes	7 Threats
4 Games	8 Force

2. Is this statement true or false? Most sexual abusers are strangers to their victims. False. A sexual abuser can be a stranger or even someone the victim knows and loves.

3. Is sexual abuse always against the law? Yes! Anyone who sexually abuses another person is breaking the law.

4. If someone wants to expose his private parts to you, what can you say? NO!

5. What are some other ways to say, "No!"? "Don't do that." "I don't want to." "I'm not supposed to do this." "I'm going to tell on you if you don't stop." Also, with actions such as screaming, yelling, or running away.

6. Is this statement true or false? If you have been sexually abused, is it a good idea to keep it a secret and hope your bad feelings about it go away? False. Tell someone you trust about it immediately.

7. Is a victim of sexual abuse partly to blame for the crime that was committed? No. The victim is not to blame. The sexual abuser is the person who broke the law and is to blame for the abuse.

8. Who has the right to keep their bodies safe? We all have the right to keep our bodies safe.

PART III

Abuse and Neglect

Child abuse and neglect are widespread problems found in all geographic areas and at every economic level in America. Parents who love and care for their children at home are faced with the danger of abuse and neglect of their children away from home. It is not enough for parents to protect their own children from this national disgrace which takes an overwhelming toll on society. Each and every one of us suffers from the lost potential of children damaged by child abuse. Knowledge of child abuse and neglect in our society is vital to combat the danger.

Emotional abuse is the most difficult to define because it is intangible.

WHAT IS ABUSE AND NEGLECT?

The National Committee for Prevention of Child Abuse divides child abuse into the following categories:

1. Nonaccidental physical injury.
2. Neglect, i.e., failure to provide a child with the necessities of life, such as food, shelter, clothing, and medical care.
3. Emotional abuse. This is the most difficult category to define because it is intangible. Generally, it is the chronic expression of a negative attitude toward a child by a parent or caretaker. A negative attitude can be expressed in many ways, such as verbal assault and the withholding of love.
4. Sexual abuse (see Part II).

Statistical Summaries on Child Abuse and Neglect (Figures are for 1982 compiled by the American Humane Association.)

- 1.3 million children were reported abused in 1982 (Figures for the following year are expected to be higher).
  - 62% experienced deprivation of necessities;
  - 17% had minor physical injuries;
  - 10% were reported emotionally abused;
  - 7% were sexually abused;
  - 2% suffered major physical injury.
- Between 2,000 and 5,000 children die each year as a direct result of child abuse. Child fatalities and severe injury were more often associated with neglect than with physical abuse.

Child fatalities and severe injury are more often associated with neglect than with physical abuse.

- 95% of the perpetrators were parents; 4% relatives; 3% nonrelatives.
- 39% of the perpetrators were male; 61% were female.
- Females were reported in higher numbers of neglect cases.
- 50% of the abused children were living with both parents; 43% were living with a single female parent.
- Most of the reported families were experiencing stresses related to health, finances, and/or family interaction.
- The average age of the abused or neglected child was 7.
- Male and female children were reported approximately equally as victims.
- 48% of the abuse reports came from nonprofessionals.

Effects of Child Abuse and Neglect

Victims. The effects of child abuse can be devastating and far reaching. Research is lacking on the long-term effects of child abuse. However, examination and treatment of victims indicate some consistencies in the effects of all types of abuse and injuries which are characteristic of particular abuses. Child abuse and neglect may result in one or more of the following effects:

- victim mortality
- impairment of growth and development
- acute and chronic medical problems
- psychiatric disorders
- multiple personality disorder
- self-destructive behavior

Poor parenting skills may predispose an adult to child abuse.

- domestic violence
- sexual dysfunction
- school failure
- negative self-image

Society. The impact of child abuse on society is incalculable in dollars and cents. Significantly, 90 percent of the inmates of correctional institutions report being abused as children. Child abuse is a major cause of psychological, social, and sexual dysfunction. Unquestionably, society pays a high monetary price for child abuse, but the greatest cost may be in the lost potential for individual fulfillment and national enrichment.

Causes of Child Abuse

Within the Family. The causes of this tragic social problem within the family can be traced to three general sources:

1. social factors
2. personal factors
3. circumstances

There are several *social factors* which contribute to the problem of child abuse:

- A social heritage that:

  1. protected the sovereignty of the family;
  2. gave absolute authority to the father over his family;
  3. defined children as the property of their parents.

- A strong traditional belief in the value of corporal punishment.

Alcoholism may predispose an adult to child abuse.

- Economic recession.
- The prevalence of violence in our society.

Personal factors which may predispose to child abuse are:

- experiencing abuse as a child
- violence between spouses
- strong belief in corporal punishment
- parental failure to bond with an infant
- poor coping skills
- poor parenting skills
- alcoholism and drug abuse

Circumstances which may contribute to child abuse potential are:

- Isolation. Abusive families tend to socially and physically isolate themselves. This inhibits both support and detection.
- Unemployment or financial stress.
- Marital problems.
- Age or characteristics of the child. The heaviest incidence of abuse and neglect is among children from birth to four years of age, and those with birth defects or developmental problems.

Child abuse is seldom the result of a single factor, but a combination of social and personal factors aggravated by circumstances.

Outside the Family. The child care needs of parents are more frequently being met by private facilities which are attempting to fill the void left by governmental cut-

Child abuse is seldom the result of a single factor, but a combination of social and personal factors aggravated by circumstances.

backs and industry's reluctance to respond to parents' needs. Athletic and recreational programs also place children under the supervision of nonfamily adults or teenagers in programs away from home.

News reports of abuse have confronted parents with the startling realization that our children can be safe and well cared for at home, and abused or neglected away from home.

SEEKING SOLUTIONS TO THE PROBLEM OF ABUSE AND NEGLECT

Guidelines for Selecting Supervision Outside the Family

Evaluate the child care facility before you enroll your child. Suggestions for evaluating a facility are found in Part II, p. 62.
Be careful when you select the adults who surround your children (i.e., baby sitters, teachers, counselors, etc.). Choose adults who:

- are in good physical health
- are in good mental health
- have been equipped by education, training, and/or experience to work with children
- are responsible
- are sensitive, kind, and caring
- can relate to your children and will have a positive influence on them
- are people your children can relate to and will respond to
- have a genuine concern for your children's safety and well-being

Our children can be safe and well cared for at home, and abused or neglected away from home.

Before you get your children involved with an adult, do the following:

Step 1. Interview or observe the adult in action.
Step 2. Talk to people who know the adult.
Step 3. Have your children spend time with the adult.
Step 4. Have your children help you decide whether or not they should get involved with the adult.

Be Careful When You Select the Programs That Your Children Participate In

Supervision. No group of children should be left without adult supervision at any time. There should be at least one adult for every:

- 2 infants
- 4 toddlers
- 5 three- to four-year-olds
- 7 four- to six-year-olds
- 10 six- to twelve-year-olds

Enrollment. For proper management, a group should be no larger than:

- 4 infants
- 8 toddlers
- 15 three- to four-year-olds
- 25–30 six- to twelve-year-olds

Facilities. The facilities should be safe, clean, and well maintained. There should be at least one toilet and one sink for every fourteen children. Drinking water must be readily available to the children.

Indoor Space. There should be approximately thirty-five square feet of indoor space per child.

Outdoor Space. There should be approximately seventy-five square feet of outdoor space per child. This space should be a safe place for children and should provide adequate amounts of sunshine and shade.

Play Equipment and Materials. There should be a sufficient variety and quantity of play equipment and materials to meet the interests and needs of the children.

Activities. The activities provided by the program should be safe as well as enriching.

The Schedule. The schedule should involve adequate amounts of physical activity. Generally speaking, young children should not do passive activities, (i.e., sitting and listening) for more than ten to twenty minutes at a time. Older children should not do passive activities for more than fifteen to thirty minutes at a time. The schedule should also involve rest or restful activities. In general, children should rest or do restful activities for at least one and a half hours of a six-hour day.

Discipline. Discipline should be reasonable as well as consistent. Constructive methods should be used for maintaining group control and individual behavior. Corporal punishment and other humiliating or frightening techniques should not be used. Punishment should never be associated with water, food, rest, or toilet privileges.

Parent Participation. Parents should be allowed and encouraged to observe the program any time, and as often as they feel a need to do so.

Identifying Abuse and Neglect

Your Own Child. Your child's behavior is the best indicator of possible problems in child care. Watch for signs that may indicate abuse. These include:

- regressive behavior, such as thumbsucking or bed-wetting
- nightmares or sleep disturbances
- loss of appetite
- extreme anxiety symptoms
- expressed fear of going to child care or associating with a particular person
- change in attitude or performance in school
- physical signs, such as: redness around the genital area, genital irritation, underpants worn inside out, genital or rectal bleeding, or unexplained bruises

If your child tells you about an abuse experience of his or her own, or that of another child, take action by doing the following:

- Do not return your child to that caretaker.
- Check with other parents of children who use the same caretaker.
- Confront the accused caretaker with your child's report, but *not* in the child's presence.
- If you still suspect abuse, report the caretaker or the center to the nearest child protective service (see "Reporting Child Abuse" on p. 87).
- Follow up on your report to see that appropriate action has been taken.

Other Children. Indications of possible physical abuse, neglect, or emotional maltreatment are:

- unexplained injuries indicated by bruises, fractures, lacerations, or abrasions in various stages of healing
- consistently untreated medical or dental problems
- consistent lack of supervision
- persistent hunger
- inappropriate dress

Early detection and reporting is essential to intervention at the earliest possible stages of abuse or neglect.

- poor hygiene
- poor physical and/or social development
- reluctance of child to be at home

Early detection and reporting is essential to intervention at the earliest possible stages of abuse or neglect.

Reporting Child Abuse

Child protection agencies depend upon third party reporting for their intervention in child abuse cases. Although reporting statutes vary from state to state, all states have the following practices in common:

1. All fifty states require certain professionals to report suspected child abuse.
2. Any individual reporting child abuse, whether by legal requirement or voluntarily, is granted immunity from civil or criminal liability.
3. Each state has a designated agency for receiving and investigating suspected child abuse.

To report a suspected case of child abuse, notify the designated agency in the state where the child lives. The agency is listed in the telephone directory under one of these headings:

State Department of:

- Social Services
- Protective Services
- Children and Family Services

For assistance in locating the agency in your community, contact your local police services or phone Childhelp USA: (800) 422–4453 for nationwide listings of protective service agencies. Include in your report the following information:

- child's name
- child's current whereabouts
- type and extent of the abuse
- child's age
- address of the child's parents or guardians

You can obtain a copy of your state's child abuse reporting statute from your local:

- Department of Social Service
- Law enforcement agency
- District Attorney's office
- Regional office of Child Development (Department of Health and Human Services)

Child Abuse Prevention

In Your Home. Be sure that you do not get to a point where you might abuse your children. To prevent child abuse in your home, follow these guidelines for responsible parenting:

- Learn how to be a responsible caretaker of children.
- Learn what you can realistically expect from children. Avoid expecting too much.

You can learn these things by talking to other adults, reading, attending classes, etc.

Assume responsibility for getting your own needs met. Do not expect your children to do this for you.

Get professional help if you:

- are continually frustrated
- feel overwhelmed
- have unresolved childhood trauma
- are addicted to drugs or alcohol
- allow your emotions, rather than your child's behavior, to dictate your use of discipline

Be sure that you do not allow your children to be neglected. Get help if you feel that you are unable to meet your children's physical, emotional, or educational needs. Help is available for parents in crisis by calling:

Parents Anonymous
In California (800) 352–0386
Outside of California (800) 421–0353

Nationally. To join the nationwide movement to eliminate child abuse, contact these organizations for information:

- The American Humane Association
  Children's Division
  9725 East Hampden Avenue
  Denver, Colorado 80231
  (303) 695–0811
- National Committee for Prevention of Child Abuse
  332 South Michigan Avenue, Suite 1250
  Chicago, Illinois 60604–4357
  (312) 663–3520

Locally. Combat child abuse in your community by volunteering your help to families in need. Be sensitive to the needs of troubled and needy families by offering your time to:

- share parenting responsibilities;
- act as surrogate family member—grandparent, aunt, uncle, big sister or brother to children who need adult attention;
- provide encouragement and support for both parents and children.

Support organized volunteer programs in your community to help prevent child abuse, such as:

- Foster Grandparents sponsored by ACTION, a national volunteer agency.
- Big Brothers and Big Sisters of America.
- YMCA and YWCA
- Boy's Clubs of America.

Protect Your Child

The best protection against child abuse is a child's

- communication with his or her parents, and
- education about child abuse.

Maintain open communication with your child. Be accessible to questions and disclosures with a nonjudgmental attitude.

To educate your child about the dangers of child abuse, use *Abuse and Neglect: Alerting Kids to the Danger Zones.* To maximize the book's benefits for your child, do the following:

- Read the book with your child.
- Listen for questions, concerns, and responses to the material.
- Answer your child's questions with a confident, matter-of-fact attitude.

Safety Zones Comprehension Test
(Parent's Answer Key)

Part III—Abuse and Neglect

1. How old is a person who is a minor? People are minors when they are any age from birth to eighteen years old.
2. Who has the responsibility for the care of minors? Adults are responsible for the care of minors.
3. Why do adults use discipline with minors? To help minors avoid misbehaving. To help minors learn the correct way to act.
4. What is it called when adults overdo discipline with minors? When adults overdo discipline, it can result in physical or emotional abuse.
5. What is neglect? Neglect is when adults fail to give minors the things they need to survive and grow.
6. How can you know for sure the difference between discipline and abuse? It is hard to decide these things by yourself. Ask a caring adult to help you determine whether you or someone you know has been abused or neglected.
7. What is the best way to help a friend who is being abused or neglected? If you think your friend is being abused or neglected, encourage your friend to talk to caring adults. You may also want to talk to adults about the situation to make sure that your friend gets help.
8. If your report of abuse is ignored by the adult you talk to, what can you do? Keep talking to people until you find someone to help you.

Resources for Child Abuse and Missing Children

Adam Walsh Child Resource Center
Mercede Executive Park
Park View Building, Suite 306
1876 N. University Dr.
Fort Lauderdale, FL 33322
(305) 475–4847

The American Humane Association
Children's Division
9725 E. Hampden Ave.
Denver, CO 80231
(303) 695–0811

American Red Cross
17th and D Streets, N.W.
Washington, D.C. 20006
(202) 737–8300

Association for Volunteer Administration
P.O. Box 4584
Boulder, CO 80302
(303) 497–0238

Association of Junior Leagues
825 Third Ave.
New York, NY 10022
(212) 355–4380

Bay Area Center for Victims of Child Stealing
1165 Meridian Ave., Suite 112
San Jose, CA 95125
(408) 247–0195

Big Brothers/Big Sisters of America
117 S. 17th St.
Suite 1200
Philadelphia, PA 19103
(215) 567-2748

Boy Scouts of America, Inc.
P.O. Box 61030
Dallas/Ft. Worth Airport, TX 75261
(214) 659-2000

Boys Club of America
771 First Ave.
New York, NY 10017
(212) 557-7755

CampFire, Inc.
4601 Madison Ave.
Kansas City, MO 64112
(816) 756-1950

C. Henry Kempe National Center for the Prevention &
Treatment of Child Abuse and Neglect
1205 Oneida
Denver, CO 80220

Child Assault Prevention Project
P.O. Box 02084
Columbus, OH 43202

Child Abuse Information Center
3727 W. 6th St., Suite 507
Los Angeles, CA 90020

Child Find
P.O. Box 277
New Paltz, NY 12561
(914) 255-1848
(800) 431-5005

Child Sexual Abuse and Diagnostic and Treatment
Center
Children's Institute International
Los Angeles, CA

Child Welfare League of America
67 Irving Place
New York, NY 10003
(215) 254-7410

Children's Defense Fund
122 C St., N.W.
Washington, D.C. 20001
(202) 628-8787

Children's Legal Rights Information and Training
2008 Hillyer Place, N.W.
Washington, D.C. 20009
(202) 332-6575

Children's Rights Group
693 Mission St.
San Francisco, CA 20009
(202) 332-6575

Coalition for Child Advocacy
P.O. Box 159
Bellingham, WA 98227

Community Advocates for Safety & Self Reliance
4183 S.E. Division
Portland, OR 97202

Day Care Council of America
1602 17th St., N.W.
Washington, D.C. 20036
(202) 745–0220

Family Violence Research Program
University of New Hampshire
Durham, NH 03824
Attn: David Finkelhor

Find the Children
11811 W. Olympic Blvd.
Los Angeles, CA 90064
(800) KID–FIND

Foundation for America's Sexually Exploited Children,
Inc.
2501 Crest Dr.
Bakersfield, CA 93306

Girl Scouts of the U.S.A.
830 Third Ave.
New York, NY 10022
(212) 940–7500

Girls Clubs of America
205 Lexington Ave.
New York, NY 10016
(212) 689–3700

Illusion Theater (TOUCH)
Sexual Abuse Prevention Program
Hennepin Center for the Arts
528 Hennepin Ave., Suite 205
Minneapolis, MN 55403

K-I-D Program
P.O. Box 6770
Kansas City, MO 64123
(816) 483–7598

National Assembly of National Voluntary Health and
Social Welfare Organizations
291 Broadway
New York, NY 10007
(212) 267–1700

National Association for Child Care Management
1800 M St., N.W.
Suite 1030N
Washington, D.C. 20036
(202) 452–8100

National Association of County Human Services
Administrators
c/o National Association of Counties
1735 New York Ave., N.W.
Washington, D.C. 20006
(202) 783–5113

National Association of Girls Clubs
5808 16th St., N.W.
Washington, D.C. 20011
(202) 726–2044

National Center for Missing and Exploited Children
1835 K St., N.W.
Suite 700
Washington, D.C. 20006
(800) 843–5678

National Center on Child Abuse and Neglect
Department of Health and Human Services
Administration for Children, Youth, and Families
P.O. Box 1182
Washington, D.C. 20013
(202) 245–2856

National Child Identification Center, Inc.
P.O. Box 3068
Albuquerque, NM 87190
(800) 222–4453

National Committee for Prevention of Child Abuse
332 S. Michigan Ave.
Suite 1250
Chicago, IL 60604–4357
(312) 663–3520

National Legal Resource Center for Child Advocacy and
Protection
c/o American Bar Association
1800 M St., N.W.
Washington, D.C. 20036
(202) 331–2250

Parents Anonymous
22330 Hawthorne Blvd.
Torrance, CA 90505
In California (800) 352–0386
Outside California (800) 421–0353

Parents United—Child Help U.S.A.
P.O. Box 952
San Jose, CA 95108
(800) 422–4453

Parents without Partners
7910 Woodmont Ave.
Suite 1000
Washington, D.C. 20014
(202) 654–8850

Region X Child Abuse/Neglect Resource Center
157 Yesler Way, #208
Seattle, WA 98104

San Francisco Child Abuse Council
4093 24th St.
San Francisco, CA 94114

Save the Children Federation
54 Wilton Rd.
Westport, CT 06880
(203) 226–7271

Sonoma County Council of Child Abuse & Neglect
1030 Second St. (Rear)
Santa Rosa, CA 95404

V.O.I.C.E.S., Inc.
Victims of Incest Can Emerge Survivors
P.O. Box 148309
Chicago, IL 60614

Volunteer: The National Center for Citizen Involvement
P.O. Box 4179
Boulder, CO 80306
(303) 447–0492

Young Men's Christian Associations of the United States
101 North Wacker Dr.
Chicago, IL 60606
(312) 977–0031

Young Women's Christian Associations of the United
States of America
600 Lexington Ave.
New York, NY 10022
(212) 753–4700

The names and addresses of child protective services agencies for each state are listed below, along with the procedures for reporting suspected child abuse. (Provided by the National Center on Child Abuse and Neglect.)

Alabama:
  Alabama Department of Pensions and Security
  64 North Union
  Montgomery, AL 36130

  Reports made to county 24-hour emergency telephone services.

Alaska:
  Department of Health and Social Services
  Division of Family and Youth
  Services
  Pouch H-05
  Juneau, AK 99811

  Reports made to Division of Social Services field offices.

American Samoa:
  Government of American Samoa
  Office of the Attorney General
  Pago Pago, AS 96799

  Reports made to the Department of Medical Services.

Arizona:
  Department of Economic Security
  P.O. Box 6123
  Phoenix, AZ 85005

  Reports made to Department of Economic Security local offices.

Arkansas:
  Arkansas Department of Human Services
  Social Services Division
  P.O. Box 1437
  Little Rock, AR 72203

  Reports made to the statewide toll-free hotline (800) 482–5964.

California:
  Department of Social Services
  714–744 P St.
  Sacramento, CA 95814

  Reports made to County Departments of Welfare and the General Registry of Child Abuse (916) 445–7546 maintained by the Department of Justice.

Colorado:
  Department of Social Services
  1575 Sherman St.
  Denver, CO 80203

  Reports made to County Departments of Social Services.

Connecticut:
  Connecticut Department of Children and Youth Services
  Division of Children and Youth Services
  170 Sigourney St.
  Hartford, CT 06105

  Reports made to (800) 842–2288.

Delaware:
Delaware Department of Health and Social Services
Division of Social Services
P.O. Box 309
Wilmington, DE 19899

Reports made to statewide toll-free reporting hotline
(800) 292–9582.

District of Columbia:
District of Columbia Department of Human Services
Commission on Social Services
Family Services Administration
Child Protective Services Division
First and I Sts., N.W.
Washington, DC 20024

Reports made to (202) 727–0995.

Florida:
Florida Department of Health and Rehabilitative
Services
1317 Winewood Blvd.
Tallahassee, FL 32301

Reports made to (800) 342–9152.

Georgia:
Georgia Department of Human Resources
47 Trinity Ave., S.W.
Atlanta, GA 30334

Reports made to County Departments of Family and
Children Services.

Guam:
  Child Welfare Services
  Child Protective Services
  P.O. Box 2816
  Agana, CU 96910

  Reports made to the State Child Protective Services
  Agency at (202) 646–8417.

Hawaii:
  Department of Social Services and Housing
  Public Welfare Division
  Family and Children's Services
  P.O. Box 339
  Honolulu, HI 96809

  Reports made to the hotline operated by Kapiolani—
  Children's Medical Center on Oahu, and to branch
  offices of the Division of Hawaii, Maui, Kauai, Mokalai.

Idaho:
  Department of Health and Welfare
  Child Protection
  Division of Welfare
  Statehouse
  Boise, ID 83702

  Reports made to Department of Health and Welfare
  Regional Offices.

Illinois:
  Illinois Department of Children and Family Services
  State Administrative Offices
  One North Old State Capitol Plaza
  Springfield, IL 62706

  Reports made to (800) 25–ABUSE.

Indiana:
Indiana Department of Public Welfare
Division of Child Welfare—Social Services
141 South Meridian Street, 6th Floor
Indianapolis, IN 46225

Reports made to County Departments of Public
Welfare.

Iowa:
Iowa Department of Social Services
Division of Community Programs
Hoover State Office Building
Fifth Floor
Des Moines, IA 50319

Reports made to the legally mandated toll-free
reporting hotline (800) 362–2178.

Kansas:
Kansas Department of Social and Rehabilitation
Services
Division of Social Services
Child Protection and Family Services Section
Smith-Wilson Building
2700 W. Sixth
Topeka, KS 66606

Reports made to Department of Social and
Rehabilitation Services Area Offices.

Kentucky:
Kentucky Department for Human Resources
275 E. Main St.
Frankfort, KY 40621

Reports made to County Offices within four regions
of the state.

Louisiana:

Louisiana Department of Health and Human
Resources
Office of Human Development
Baton Rouge, LA 70804

Reports made to the parish protective service units.

Maine:

Maine Department of Human Services
Human Services Building
Augusta, ME 04333

Reports made to Regional Office or to State Agency
at (800) 452–1999.

Maryland:

Maryland Department of Human Resources
Social Services Administration
300 W. Preston St.
Baltimore, MD 21201

Reports made to County Departments of Social
Services or to local law enforcement agencies.

Massachusetts:

Massachusetts Department of Social Services
Protective Services
150 Causeway St.
Boston, MA 02114

Reports made to Regional Offices.

Michigan:

Michigan Department of Social Services
300 S. Capitol Ave.
Lansing, MI 48926

Reports made to County Departments of Social
Welfare.

Minnesota:
Minnesota Department of Public Welfare
Centennial Office Building
St. Paul, MN 55155

Reports made to the County Department of Public
Welfare.

Mississippi:
Mississippi Department of Public Welfare
Division of Social Services
P.O. Box 352
Jackson, MS 39216

Reports made to (800) 222–8000.

Missouri:
Missouri Department of Social Services
Division of Family Services
Broadway Building
Jefferson City, MO 65101

Reports made to (800) 392–3738.

Montana:
Department of Social and Rehabilitation Services
Social Services Bureau
P.O. Box 4210
Helena, MT 59601

Reports made to County Departments of Social and
Rehabilitation Services.

Nebraska:
Nebraska Department of Public Welfare
301 Centennial Mall South
5th Floor
Lincoln, NE 68509

Reports made to local law enforcement agencies or to
County Divisions of Public Welfare.

Nevada:
Department of Human Resources
Division of Welfare
251 Jeanell Dr.
Carson City, NV 89710

Reports made to Division of Welfare local offices.

New Hampshire:
New Hampshire Department of Health and Welfare
Division of Welfare
Bureau of Child and Family Services
Hazen Dr.
Concord, NH 03301

Reports made to Division of Welfare District Offices.

New Jersey:
New Jersey Division of Youth and Family Services
P.O. Box 510
One S. Montgomery St.
Trenton, NJ 08625

Reports made to (800) 792–8610.
District Offices also provide 24-hour telephone service.

New Mexico:
New Mexico Department of Human Services
P.O. Box 2348
Santa Fe, NM 87503

Reports made to County Social Offices or to (800) 432–6217.

New York:
New York Department of Social Services
Child Protective Services
40 N. Pearl St.
Albany, NY 12207

Reports made to (800) 342–3720 or to District Offices.

North Carolina:
  North Carolina Department of Human Resources
  Division of Social Services
  325 N. Salisbury St.
  Raleigh, NC 27611

  Reports made to County Departments of Social
  Services.

North Dakota:
  North Dakota Department of Human Services
  Social Services Division
  Children and Family Services Unit
  Child Abuse and Neglect Program
  Russel Building, Hwy. 83
  North Bismarck, ND 58505

  Reports made to Board of Social Services Area Offices
  and to 24-hour reporting services provided by Human
  Service Centers.

Ohio:
  Ohio Department of Public Welfare
  Bureau of Children Services
  Children's Protective Services
  30 E. Broad St.
  Columbus, OH 43215

  Reports made to County Departments of Public
  Welfare.

Oklahoma:
  Oklahoma Department of Institutions, Social and
  Rehabilitative Services
  Division of Social Services
  P.O. Box 25352
  Oklahoma City, OK 73125

  Reports made to (800) 522–3511.

Oregon:
Department of Human Resources
Children's Services Division
Protective Services
509 Public Services Building
Salem, OR 97310

Reports made to local Children's Services Division
Offices and to (503) 378–3016.

Pennsylvania:
Pennsylvania Department of Public Welfare
Office of Children, Youth and Families
Bureau of Family and Community Programs
1514 N. 2nd St.
Harrisburg, PA 17102

Reports made to the toll-free CHILDLINE (800) 932–
0313.

Puerto Rico:
Puerto Rico Department of Social Services
Services to Families With Children
P.O. Box 11398,
Fernandez Juncos Station
Santurce, PR 00910

Reports made to local offices or to the Department.

Rhode Island:
Rhode Island Department for Children and Their
Families
610 Mt. Pleasant Ave.
Providence, RI 02908

Reports made to State agency child protective services
unit at (800) 662–5100 or to District Offices.

South Carolina:
South Carolina Department of Social Services
P.O. Box 1520
Columbia SC 29202

Reports made to County Departments of Social
Services.

South Dakota:
Department of Social Services
Office of Children, Youth and Family Services
Richard F. Kneip Building
Pierre, SD 57501

Reports made to local offices.

Tennessee:
Tennessee Department of Human Services
State Office Building
Room 410
Nashville, TN 37219

Reports made to County Departments of Human
Services.

Texas:
Texas Department of Human Resources
Protective Services for Children Branch
P.O. Box 2960
Austin, TX 78701

Reports made to (800) 252–5400.

Utah:
Department of Social Services
Division of Family Services
150 West North Temple, Room 370
P.O. Box 2500
Salt Lake City, UT 84103

Reports made to Division of Family Services District
Offices.

Vermont:
Vermont Department of Social and Rehabilitative
Services
Social Services Division
103 S. Main St.
Waterbury, VT 05676

Reports made to State Agency at (802) 828–3433 or
to District Offices (24-hour services).

Virgin Islands:
Virgin Islands Department of Social Welfare
Division of Social Services
P.O. Box 500
Charlotte Amalie
St. Thomas, VI 00801

Reports made to the Division of Social Services.

Virginia:
Virginia Department of Welfare
Bureau of Family and Community Programs
Blair Building
8007 Discovery Dr.
Richmond, VA 23288

Reports made to (800) 552–7096 in Virginia, and (804)
281–9081 outside the state.

Washington:
Department of Social and Health Services
Community Services Division
Child Protective Services
Mail Stop OB 41-D
Olympia, WA 98504

Reports made to local Social and Health Services Offices.

West Virginia:
Department of Welfare
Division of Social Services
Child Protective Services
State Office Building
1900 Washington St. E.
Charleston, WV 25305

Reports made to (800) 352–6513.

Wisconsin:
Wisconsin Department of Health and Social Services
Division of Community Services
1 W. Wilson St.
Madison, WI 53702

Reports made to County Social Services Offices.

Wyoming:
Department of Health and Social Services
Division of Public Assistance and Social Services
Hathaway Building
Cheyenne, WY 82002

Reports made to County Departments of Public Assistance and Social Services.

Whereabouts Form

WHERE ARE YOU, _____ ?
                    (child's name)

Today is: Mon.   Tues.   Wed.   Thurs.   Fri.   Sat.   Sun.
           the _____ day of _____ , 19_____ .

When did you leave (time)? _____

Where will you be? _____

Phone _____

How will you get there?
   Walk __ Ride your bike __ Car __ Bus __

Who will take you? _____

Who will pick you up? _____

Who is with you? _____

How are you returning? _____

When will you be home? _____

Whereabouts Form

WHERE ARE YOU, _____ ?
                              (child's name)

Today is: Mon.   Tues.   Wed.   Thurs.   Fri.   Sat.   Sun.
            the _____ day of _____ , 19_____ .

When did you leave (time)? _____

Where will you be? _____

Phone _____

How will you get there?
    Walk __ Ride your bike __ Car __ Bus __

Who will take you? _____

Who will pick you up? _____

Who is with you? _____

How are you returning? _____

When will you be home? _____

Whereabouts Form

WHERE ARE YOU, _____ ?
                        (child's name)

Today is: Mon.   Tues.   Wed.   Thurs.   Fri.   Sat.   Sun.
           the _____ day of _____ , 19_____ .

When did you leave (time)? _____

Where will you be? _____

Phone _____

How will you get there?
    Walk __ Ride your bike __ Car __ Bus __

Who will take you? _____

Who will pick you up? _____

Who is with you? _____

How are you returning? _____

When will you be home? _____

Whereabouts Form

WHERE ARE YOU, _____ ?
(child's name)

Today is: Mon.   Tues.   Wed.   Thurs.   Fri.   Sat.   Sun.
the _____ day of _____ , 19_____ .

When did you leave (time)? _____

Where will you be? _____

Phone _____

How will you get there?
Walk __ Ride your bike __ Car __ Bus __

Who will take you? _____

Who will pick you up? _____

Who is with you? _____

How are you returning? _____

When will you be home? _____

Whereabouts Form

WHERE ARE YOU, _____ ?
(child's name)

Today is: Mon.   Tues.   Wed.   Thurs.   Fri.   Sat.   Sun.
the _____ day of _____ , 19_____ .

When did you leave (time)? _____

Where will you be? _____

Phone _____

How will you get there?
Walk __ Ride your bike __ Car __ Bus __

Who will take you? _____

Who will pick you up? _____

Who is with you? _____

How are you returning? _____

When will you be home? _____

Whereabouts Form

WHERE ARE YOU, _____ ?
                        (child's name)

Today is: Mon.   Tues.   Wed.   Thurs.   Fri.   Sat.   Sun.
        the _____ day of _____ , 19_____ .

When did you leave (time)? _____

Where will you be? _____

Phone _____

How will you get there?
  Walk __ Ride your bike __ Car __ Bus __

Who will take you? _____

Who will pick you up? _____

Who is with you? _____

How are you returning? _____

When will you be home? _____

Whereabouts Form

WHERE ARE YOU, _____ ?
                          (child's name)

Today is: Mon.   Tues.   Wed.   Thurs.   Fri.   Sat.   Sun.
            the _____ day of _____ , 19_____ .

When did you leave (time)? _____

Where will you be? _____

Phone _____

How will you get there?
  Walk __ Ride your bike __ Car __ Bus __

Who will take you? _____

Who will pick you up? _____

Who is with you? _____

How are you returning? _____

When will you be home? _____

Whereabouts Form

WHERE ARE YOU, _____ ?
                        (child's name)

Today is: Mon.   Tues.   Wed.   Thurs.   Fri.   Sat.   Sun.
           the _____ day of _____ , 19_____ .

When did you leave (time)? _____

Where will you be? _____

Phone _____

How will you get there?
    Walk __ Ride your bike __ Car __ Bus __

Who will take you? _____

Who will pick you up? _____

Who is with you? _____

How are you returning? _____

When will you be home? _____

Emergency Information Form

Information updated: _____ (date)
Full Name _____ Nickname _____
Address _____
City, State, Zip _____
Telephone number _____
Place of Birth _____ Date of Birth _____
Sex _____ Nationality/Race _____
Height _____ Weight _____ Hair color _____ Eye color _____
Complexion color _____ Right or Left handed? _____
Identification marks _____
_____ .

Physical handicaps _____
Past injuries _____
_____ .

Allergies _____
Medications currently being taken _____
_____ .

Glasses or contact lenses? _____ Braces? _____
Are any of child's teeth false or missing? _____
Other information _____
_____
_____ .

Schools Attended _____
Churches Attended _____
Doctor _____ Address _____ Phone _____
Dentist _____ Address _____ Phone _____
Other pertinent contacts:
Name _____ Phone _____ Relationship _____
Address _____
Name _____ Phone _____ Relationship _____
Address _____
Name _____ Phone _____ Relationship _____
Address _____

Attached dated photograph, fingerprints and palmprints.
Update information every six months for children under 12
and every one year for older children.

Emergency Information Form

Information updated: _____ (date)
Full Name _____ Nickname _____
Address _____
City, State, Zip _____
Telephone number _____
Place of Birth _____ Date of Birth _____
Sex _____ Nationality/Race _____
Height _____ Weight _____ Hair color _____ Eye color _____
Complexion color _____ Right or Left handed? _____
Identification marks _____
_____.
Physical handicaps _____
Past injuries _____
_____.
Allergies _____
Medications currently being taken _____
_____.
Glasses or contact lenses? _____ Braces? _____
Are any of child's teeth false or missing? _____
Other information _____
_____
_____.
Schools Attended _____
Churches Attended _____
Doctor _____ Address _____ Phone _____
Dentist _____ Address _____ Phone _____
Other pertinent contacts:
Name _____ Phone _____ Relationship _____
Address _____
Name _____ Phone _____ Relationship _____
Address _____
Name _____ Phone _____ Relationship _____
Address _____

Attached dated photograph, fingerprints and palmprints.
Update information every six months for children under 12
and every one year for older children.

Emergency Information Form

Information updated: _____ (date)
Full Name _____ Nickname _____
Address _____
City, State, Zip _____
Telephone number _____
Place of Birth _____ Date of Birth _____
Sex _____ Nationality/Race _____
Height _____ Weight _____ Hair color _____ Eye color _____
Complexion color _____ Right or Left handed? _____
Identification marks _____
_____ .

Physical handicaps _____
Past injuries _____
_____ .

Allergies _____
Medications currently being taken _____
_____ .

Glasses or contact lenses? _____ Braces? _____
Are any of child's teeth false or missing? _____
Other information _____
_____
_____ .

Schools Attended _____
Churches Attended _____
Doctor _____ Address _____ Phone _____
Dentist _____ Address _____ Phone _____
Other pertinent contacts:
Name _____ Phone _____ Relationship _____
Address _____
Name _____ Phone _____ Relationship _____
Address _____
Name _____ Phone _____ Relationship _____
Address _____

Attached dated photograph, fingerprints and palmprints.
Update information every six months for children under 12
and every one year for older children.

Emergency Information Form

Information updated: _____ (date)
Full Name _____ Nickname _____
Address _____
City, State, Zip _____
Telephone number _____
Place of Birth _____ Date of Birth _____
Sex _____ Nationality/Race _____
Height _____ Weight _____ Hair color _____ Eye color _____
Complexion color _____ Right or Left handed? _____
Identification marks _____
_____ .
Physical handicaps _____
Past injuries _____
_____ .
Allergies _____
Medications currently being taken _____
_____ .
Glasses or contact lenses? _____ Braces? _____
Are any of child's teeth false or missing? _____
Other information _____
_____
_____ .
Schools Attended _____
Churches Attended _____
Doctor _____ Address _____ Phone _____
Dentist _____ Address _____ Phone _____
Other pertinent contacts:
Name _____ Phone _____ Relationship _____
Address _____
Name _____ Phone _____ Relationship _____
Address _____
Name _____ Phone _____ Relationship _____
Address _____

Attached dated photograph, fingerprints and palmprints.
Update information every six months for children under 12
and every one year for older children.

Information Card

PLEASE SEND FREE INFORMATION ABOUT:
- [ ] The LET'S TALK ABOUT SERIES by Joy Berry.
- [ ] The SURVIVAL SERIES FOR KIDS by Joy Berry.
- [ ] The READY-SET-GROW series by Joy Berry.
- [ ] The DANGER ZONES series by Joy Berry.
- [ ] Please send me the DANGER ZONES program consisting of 3 children's books, the accompanying Parent's Guide, and other reinforcement materials.
  - [ ] Check enclosed payable to WORD, DMS, Inc. for _____ program(s) at $24.95 each.
  - [ ] Charge my order to: VISA _____ Master Card for _____ program(s) at $24.95 each.
    Account # _____ Exp Date _____
    Signature _____
- [ ] Please send information about the DANGER ZONES to my friends whose names and addresses I have indicated on the reverse side.

Mr./Mrs./Ms. _____
Address _____
City _____ State _____ Zip _____
WORD DMS, Inc. Account number (if any) _____
MAIL TO: WORD DMS, Inc. 4800 West Waco Drive, Waco, Texas 76796

Information Card

PLEASE SEND FREE INFORMATION ABOUT:
☐ The LET'S TALK ABOUT SERIES by Joy Berry.
☐ The SURVIVAL SERIES FOR KIDS by Joy Berry.
☐ The READY-SET-GROW series by Joy Berry.
☐ The DANGER ZONES series by Joy Berry.
☐ Please send me the DANGER ZONES program consisting of 3 children's books, the accompanying Parent's Guide, and other reinforcement materials.
☐ Check enclosed payable to WORD, DMS, Inc. for _____ program(s) at $24.95 each.
☐ Charge my order to: VISA _____ Master Card for _____ program(s) at $24.95 each.
Account # _____ Exp Date _____
Signature _____
☐ Please send information about the DANGER ZONES to my friends whose names and addresses I have indicated on the reverse side.

Mr./Mrs./Ms. _____
Address _____
City _____ State _____ Zip _____
WORD DMS, Inc. Account number (if any) _____
MAIL TO: WORD DMS, Inc. 4800 West Waco Drive, Waco, Texas 76796

Information Card

PLEASE SEND FREE INFORMATION ABOUT:
- [ ] The LET'S TALK ABOUT SERIES by Joy Berry.
- [ ] The SURVIVAL SERIES FOR KIDS by Joy Berry.
- [ ] The READY-SET-GROW series by Joy Berry.
- [ ] The DANGER ZONES series by Joy Berry.

- [ ] Please send me the DANGER ZONES program consisting of 3 children's books, the accompanying Parent's Guide, and other reinforcement materials.
  - [ ] Check enclosed payable to WORD, DMS, Inc. for _____ program(s) at $24.95 each.
  - [ ] Charge my order to: VISA _____ Master Card for _____ program(s) at $24.95 each.
    Account # _____ Exp Date _____
    Signature _____
- [ ] Please send information about the DANGER ZONES to my friends whose names and addresses I have indicated on the reverse side.

Mr./Mrs./Ms. _____

Address _____

City _____ State _____ Zip _____

WORD DMS, Inc. Account number (if any) _____

MAIL TO: WORD DMS, Inc. 4800 West Waco Drive, Waco, Texas 76796

Information Card

PLEASE SEND FREE INFORMATION ABOUT:
- [ ] The LET'S TALK ABOUT SERIES by Joy Berry.
- [ ] The SURVIVAL SERIES FOR KIDS by Joy Berry.
- [ ] The READY-SET-GROW series by Joy Berry.
- [ ] The DANGER ZONES series by Joy Berry.
- [ ] Please send me the DANGER ZONES program consisting of 3 children's books, the accompanying Parent's Guide, and other reinforcement materials.
  - [ ] Check enclosed payable to WORD, DMS, Inc. for _____ program(s) at $24.95 each.
  - [ ] Charge my order to: VISA _____ Master Card for _____ program(s) at $24.95 each.
    Account # _____ Exp Date _____
    Signature _____
- [ ] Please send information about the DANGER ZONES to my friends whose names and addresses I have indicated on the reverse side.

Mr./Mrs./Ms. _____

Address _____

City _____ State _____ Zip _____

WORD DMS, Inc. Account number (if any) _____

MAIL TO: WORD DMS, Inc. 4800 West Waco Drive, Waco, Texas 76796

About the Authors

Joy Berry

Joy Berry is an expert on communicating with children and a firm believer in empowering kids to protect themselves. With the *Danger Zones* books, her goal is to provide children with the knowledge they need to make a decision about suspicious situations and to take action to remove themselves from danger.

Joy's books treat important issues that can be overwhelming to a child. They are designed to be fun, to encourage communication, and to be flexible enough to be used by the parent and the child together and subsequently by the child alone. With this method, Joy says, "learning to cope becomes the easy, natural offshoot of understanding."

The founder and director of the Institute of Living Skills, Joy has a bachelor's degree in biological science and a master's degree in human development. She has California state credentials in elementary education, early childhood education, and elementary administration. In her varied career, she has been a teacher, a minister, a social worker, and a school administrator as well as a consultant, writer, educator, and mother of Christopher and Lisa.

Joy has appeared as a guest on "Hour Magazine," "The Merv Griffin Show," "Good Morning New York," "Eyewitness News," "Today in New York," "Today in Chicago," "New England Today," and many more national and regional television and radio programs.

Kathleen McBride

Kathleen McBride is a free-lance writer and research anthropologist. She brings to parent education her view of the broad cultural issues which impact children, such as social change, and presents the information parents and children need to successfully cope with these issues. It is Kathleen's belief that, "a society that fails to nurture and protect its children risks disintegration."

Adult education for child advocacy is Kathleen's goal in co-authoring *A Parent's Guide to the Danger Zones.* She collaborates with co-author Joy Berry on parent education at the Institute of Living Skills in Sebastopol, California.

Kathleen and her husband Mike have educated their three children in a public school alternative program administered and taught by Mr. McBride. As the mother of two teenagers, Heidi and Michael, and their first-grader, Kelly, Kathleen is committed to parent education. "The challenge of parenting has never been greater, but so is the possibility of achieving our ideals about what childhood can be."